Friendship &
Dating Manners
for Teens

Surviving the Social Scene

D0187988

The **How Rude!™** Handbook of

Friendship & Dating Manners for Teens

Surviving the Social Scene

Alex J. Packer, Ph.D.

Edited by Pamela Espeland

free spirit
PUBLiSHiNG®

Helping kids
help themselves™
since 1983

Library of Congress Cataloging-in-Publication Data
Packer, Alex J.
  The how rude! handbook of friendship & dating manners for teens : surviving the social scene / Alex J. Packer ; edited by Pamela Espeland.
    p. cm. — (The how rude handbooks for teens)
  Includes index.
  ISBN 1-57542-165-8
 1. Etiquette for children and teenagers. 2. Friendship. 3. Dating (Social customs) I.
Espeland, Pamela. II. Title. III. Series.
  BJ1857.C5P327 2004
  395.1'23—dc22   2004018973

Cover design by Marieka Heinlen
Interior design by Percolator
Illustrations by Jeff Tolbert
Index prepared by Ina Gravitz

10 9 8 7 6 5 4 3 2
Printed in the United States of America

Free Spirit Publishing Inc.
217 Fifth Avenue North, Suite 200
Minneapolis, MN 55401-1299
(612) 338-2068
help4kids@freespirit.com
www.freespirit.com

 Printed on recycled paper
including 30%
post-consumer waste

CONTENTS

CAUTION!

This is a book about manners.

If that makes you feel like rolling
your eyes, at least say "Excuse me"
if they get stuck that way.

INTRODUCTION

Life is full of everyday dilemmas. Like:

■ Do you really have to hold up your pinkie when you drink from a teacup?

■ What do you do when you can't remember someone's name?

■ Is it rude to listen in on other people's conversations?

■ What's the best way to ask someone out?

■ What's the best way to say no if you don't want to go out with someone who asks you?

■ What can you say when a friend pressures you to do drugs?

Of course, there isn't one solution to all of those problems. But there *is* one set of guidelines that can help you come up with solutions.

What are these amazing guidelines? *Manners.* Also known as etiquette. Politeness. Protocol. Proper behavior. And not grossing people out.

The Manners Advantage

Teenagers everywhere are discovering the blessings that good manners bring. When we did a survey of teens, here's what some of them said:

"Because I am always polite and respectful, I don't get into fights."

"My family compliments me."

"Teachers respect me more."

"I get better service in restaurants."

"I have been hired for different jobs because adults are looking for kids with good manners and don't think they exist."

"When I let someone go ahead of me, a bird pooped on his head instead of mine."

And here's what happened to teenagers in our survey who DIDN'T use good manners:

"I got grounded."

"I got suspended."

"I got beat up."

"I got a bad reputation."

"I offended a good friend."

"Once I wanted my parents to let me do something and I started yelling and they said, 'We were going to let you, but not anymore.'"

Rude Things So-Called Friends Do to Each Other

PART ONE

When we asked teenagers, "What's the rudest thing anyone's ever done to you?" here's what some of them said:

Someone...

- lifted me completely into the air by my underwear.
- farted in my face while we wrestled.
- spread rumors about me.

Someone...

- told a secret about me when I told him not to.
- went through my personal things.
- only pretended to be my friend.

Someone...

- embarrassed me in front of my other friends.
- excluded me from a party just to see me suffer.
- dumped me because I wouldn't have sex with him.

For reasons unknown, some people think they can treat their friends the same way they treat their family members. They're rude. They're crude. They're thoughtless and careless. They hurt people on purpose.

With friends like these, who needs enemas?

But wait. The teens we surveyed weren't just the victims of bad behavior. When pressed, they 'fessed up to crimes of their own.

Rude Things So-Called Friends Do to Each Other

PART TWO

When we asked teenagers, "What's the rudest thing you ever did to anyone?" here's what they said:

I...

- talked about someone behind their back.
- laughed when someone got hurt.
- put a stinky sock in someone's mouth.

I...

- snubbed a couple of childhood friends for a different group of newer friends.
- called someone a fag.
- told someone she might be really pretty if she lost a lot of weight.

I...

- slammed a door in a girl's face.
- repeated a secret.
- made fun of someone only to be part of the group.

Why This Book?

Nowhere (well, almost nowhere) are manners more important than in friendship and dating relationships.

Would you like to spend your life alone in a room where the phone never rings and your computer never says, "You've got mail?" Then go right ahead and treat your friends rudely.

Do you want to make sure never, ever to meet someone who's willing to share the giant-sized popcorn with you at the movies, and who also, by the way, makes your heart beat faster? Then be a bad-mannered, selfish slob on every date, until the word gets out and no one will be seen with you.

Having good manners involves a lot more than knowing not to drink from the toilet bowl. It means knowing how to handle yourself in all kinds of situations. People who know how to handle themselves come out on top. They get what they want. They feel good about themselves. They enjoy life to the fullest. Manners, in short, are a constant source of power, pleasure, and self-confidence.

This book will help you acquire and use the manners that lead to lasting friendships, great dates, and all-around happiness.

Good luck—and good manners!

Alex Packer
Boston, Massachusetts

 **Do you really have to hold up your pinkie when you drink from a teacup?**

Times have changed, and this is no longer necessary. Just be sure not to hold up your middle finger. ◆

First Impressions

Making a new friend, asking someone out, being asked out—it all starts with meeting someone. Everyone's a stranger until that first "Hi," "Hey," "Hello," or "Yo." And, like it or not, first impressions count.

Introducing Yourself

This is the simplest introduction. All you have to do is remember your own name!

At school or parties, or when others have neglected to introduce you, look the person you want to meet in the eye, smile, hold out your right hand, and say, "Hi, I'm _____."

If the person doesn't respond with his or her name, you can say, "And you're...?" Or, "Who are you?" Or, "What's your name?"

Easy as pie.

Introducing Others

This is a bit trickier, since you have to remember other people's names.

When you're with one friend, another friend comes up to you, and you know they don't know each other, say, "Natasha, this is Boris. Boris, meet Natasha."

If you think they might know each other but you're not sure, you can turn your introduction into a question: "Natasha, have you met Boris?"

Piece of cake.

Try to include a little information about the people you're introducing. Otherwise, they may stare at their feet with nothing to say. *Examples:*

"Natasha, this is Boris. Last year, he ran the Boston Marathon."

"Boris, this is Natasha. She's a swimmer. Her coach thinks she's good enough to compete in the Olympics someday."

"Rootie, this is Tootie. He plays the trumpet."

"Tootie, this is Rootie. She's a cheerleader at Hoser High."

You can see how these add-ons provide openings for further conversation. Be discreet, though. The idea is to share an interesting bit of information, not to spill any beans.

3 Strategies to Try If You've Forgotten Someone's Name

You're talking with one friend when another approaches. Great... wait...uh-oh...oh, no! You've forgotten one of their names!

"Boris, I'd like you to meet...er, ah, um, uh..." is a poor introduction. But we all forget names sometimes. Since it's worse to make *no* introduction, you have three choices:

1. **Be up-front.** Come clean about your mental lapse. Start the introduction ("Boris, this is a friend of mine"), then turn to the other person and say, "I'm so sorry, I've temporarily forgotten your name." If you're introducing yourself, say, "Hi, we've met before, but I'm afraid I've forgotten your name. I'm _____."

   What if you're introducing two people and you've forgotten *both* of their names? The up-front approach would be, "I'm sorry. I'm so terrible with names that I'd forget my own if it wasn't sewn into my underwear. Could you two introduce yourselves?"

2. **Bluff.** Try to get people whose names you've forgotten to make their own introductions. Start by looking warmly at both of them. Then say, "Do you know each other?" If the bluff works, they will reply, "No, we haven't met. I'm Boris." "Nice to meet you Boris. I'm Natasha." If the bluff doesn't work, they will both turn to you with expectant looks. Busted! Move back to choice #1.

   If you've forgotten just one person's name, turn to that person and say, "Have you met Boris? We work out

continues...

together at the Y." With any luck, the person will reply, "No, I haven't had the pleasure. Hi, Boris, I'm Natasha."

You can even use the bluff technique when introducing *yourself* to someone whose name you've forgotten. Smile, stick out your hand, and say, "Hi. It's good to see you again. I'm _____." Then hope that person responds in kind.

3. **Cheat.** It's not nice, but sometimes it's necessary. Act frantic and invent an emergency: "Oh, dear, I think the dog just ate my gerbil!" Then say, "Could you please introduce your-selves?" as you rush from the room.

Group Introductions

Situations may arise that call for group introductions. **Example:** Your cousin joins you and some friends for a movie. If the group is small (five people or fewer), you can introduce him to everyone. If the group is large, individual introductions will take forever and you'll miss the movie. It's perfectly fine to say, "Hey, everybody, this is my cousin Alfredo Fettucine. He's visiting from Rome."

Alfredo can smile and say "Hi." The rest of you can smile and say "Hey" or "How's it goin'?" Gestures are also acceptable—a wave, a friendly salute, a tip of the baseball cap—anything that makes Alfredo feel welcome. Standing up (if you're sitting down) and shaking hands is unnecessary in such informal situations. Individual members of the group should introduce themselves to Alfredo as they talk with him throughout the evening.

SPOTLIGHT ON...

WHY PEOPLE SHAKE HANDS

You may be wondering, "Why do people shake hands?"

I once wondered the very same thing, so I went to the library and looked it up.

The ancient Egyptians believed that this was how a god transferred power to a king. (There's evidence in hieroglyphics dating back to 2800 B.C.) Michelangelo's painting *The Creation of Man* on the ceiling of the Sistine Chapel shows God reaching for Adam's hand.

Another possible reason for the handshake goes back to the days when strangers approached each other with suspicion. Men held their daggers in their right hands until they knew that no threat existed. At that point, they sheathed their daggers and held out their right hands to show friendship and goodwill. (This helps to explain why women didn't shake hands until fairly recently. Most women didn't carry daggers.)

Today, people shake hands because it's a custom. Many peer groups, sports teams, and fraternal organizations use secret or special handshakes among their members. Some of these got their start back in the Middle Ages as ways to tell friend from foe. Special handshakes are fine within peer groups, as long as they're not used to make others feel excluded.

Being Introduced

What should you do when you're being introduced? Follow these five steps:

1. **Assume the position.** If you're not already standing, stand up. Use good posture. Don't fidget or pace.

2. **Make eye contact.** Give people a friendly, welcoming look. Don't stare into space or study your shoes.

3. **Shake hands.** Use enough pressure so your hand feels like a hand, not an overcooked noodle. A confident, steady grip sends the message that you're a confident, steady person.

4. **Express a greeting.** You can't go wrong with, "How do you do?" A warm "Hello" or "Pleased to meet you" are also good. Save "Yo," "Hey," "What's happening?" and "'S'up?" for people around your age. For extra credit,

spice up your greeting with, "I've really been looking forward to meeting you," or, "My sister Sadie has told me so much about you."

5. **Make conversation.** * If the introducer did his job, he gave you a clue about the person you were just introduced to. Follow up with related questions and/or comments. Try to avoid questions that can be answered with a simple yes or no.

   Examples: If a friend introduces you to one of his teammates, you might say, "What position do you play?" or, "What are practices like?" or, "How do you think the team will do this season?" You could ask a student who's new to your school, "How do you like our town so far?" or, "What courses are you taking?" or, "What was your last school like?" or, "What clubs are you thinking of joining?"

   These aren't the world's most thrilling questions. But they do say something about you: You make an effort. You don't just stand there like a lump. And that counts for a lot. As you discover interests and experiences you have in common, your conversation will improve. Or, if the person turns out to be a bore, there are ways to bow out without being rude. **

   Starting a conversation may feel awkward at first. Just remember that most people like to talk about themselves. The more they get to do that, the more fascinating they will think *you* are.

---

* See pages 19–35 for a whole chapter on chatter.

** See page 32.

4 Strategies for Remembering People's Names

Does this sound like you? You meet people, you hear their names, and you immediately forget them. They go in one ear and out the other.

You're not alone. A lot of people have this problem. But most of them don't know the four strategies you're about to learn.

1. **Repeat the person's name.** The introducer says, "_____, meet Muriel." You immediately say, "Hi, Muriel. I'm pleased to meet you." If someone else you know is standing nearby, say, "Marco, have you met Muriel?" You've just said Muriel's name twice, which should help you to remember it.

2. **Look for an unusual feature.** Does Muriel have a mohawk? A mole? Be discreet, but look for something memorable. File it away in your mind.

3. **Come up with a mnemonic.** A mnemonic (say *ne-MON-ik*, not *me-nem-a-nom-a-neem-oh-forget-it*) is anything that helps you to remember something. Rhymes are good mnemonics. Try thinking something like, "Muriel, mercurial." If you're not quick with the rhymes, or there aren't any rhymes ("William of Orange...uh...porridge?"), try the Name Game: "Muriel bo Buriel, banana fana fo Furiel, me my mo Muriel." Not out loud or she'll think you're loony.

4. **Write it down.** As soon as you've left Muriel's company, write down her name. This doesn't mean making a quick exit just so you can do this. Spend time talking—which may give you chances to say things like, "That's so interesting, Muriel!" Or, "What's your opinion, Muriel?" Or, "You're really funny, Muriel!" Don't overdo it or she'll think you're daffy.

Special Cases

That's about it for introductions. Any questions?

"What if the person who's introducing me has forgotten my name?"

If she hesitates or asks, "Do you two know each other?" don't call her bluff. Help her out the way you'd want to be helped. Leap in with, "Hi, I'm _____."

"What do you do when you shake a person's hand and he won't let go?"

Give the person's hand one firm, final squeeze. Then withdraw your hand while continuing to keep eye contact and make conversation. This shows that you want to remove yourself from his grip, not his company.

"Is it okay to call adults by their first names?"

Only if they ask you to. Otherwise, it's "Doctor," "Mister," "Mrs.," "Miss," or Ms.," followed by their last names.

"What do you say if you're introduced to someone who's gay?"

"How do you do?"

"What do you say if you're introduced to someone who's in a wheelchair?"

"How do you do?"

"What do you say if you're introduced to someone you can't stand?"

"How do you do?"

"What do you say if you're introduced to triplets?"

"How do you do?" "How do you do?" "How do you do?"

Bonus Behavior: Pulling Rank

When it comes to making introductions, some people have "lesser" status, and others have "greater" status. You present the person of "lesser" status to the person of "greater" status. You address the person of "greater" status by saying his or her name first:

> **"Your Highness, I'd like to present Simon the Stableboy."**
> **"Warden, I'd like to introduce my cellmate, Lucky."**
> **"Professor Glockenspiel, this is my next-door neighbor, Squeaky."**

How, in a society where everyone's supposed to be equal, do you know who outranks who(m)? This chart will help you to keep things straight:

"Greater" Status	**"Lesser" Status**
adults	children
teachers	students
longtime friends	new friends
females	males
relatives	non-relatives
bosses	employees
the Queen of England	the town dogcatcher

Please don't have a fit about this status thing. It doesn't mean that royals are better than commoners, women are better than men, or adults are better than children. It's just the way things are done.

And don't worry about making a mistake. If you present whoever to whomever when whomever should have been presented to whoever, few people will notice. They'll be delighted that you made any introduction at all. And your own status will be tops in everyone's eyes.

If you have manners, won't people think you're weird?

The only people who think manners are weird don't have any. Who cares what they think? ◆

The Well-Mannered Conversation

People may meet by chance. They may be introduced by mutual friends or family members. They may meet over the Internet. But the way they get to know each other is always the same: through conversation. Following are some tips and guidelines that will make you a talented talker.

How to Start a Conversation

Lots of people feel awkward or shy when starting a conversation. That's natural. But anyone can do it if they know the secret of successful small talk, which is…sorry, it's a secret.

Oh, all right, here it is: The secret is to *ask questions*. That's all you have to do to get a conversation going. The best questions are those with open-ended answers. Questions with yes-or-no answers are okay, but they make your work harder.

Here's what happens when someone trying to start a conversation offers personal opinions and yes-or-no questions:

You: *"Great music."*

The Other Guy: *"Yeah."*

You: *"Do you like the new CD by the Empty Bladders?"*

OG: *"Yeah."*

You: *"Cool party."*

OG: *"Yeah."*

You: *"You a friend of Mike's?"*

OG: *"Yeah."*

You: *"Cool."*

Now watch how much better the conversation flows if the questions are more open-ended:

You: *"What do you think of the music?"*

OG: *"Rave totale. Compliments to the chef de musique. This DJ's waaaaay."*

You: *"Waaaaay?"*

OG: *"Yeah, you know. Waaaaay. He was the spinologist at another festivity I went to last weekend. Total Empty Bladders freak, this guy."*

You: *"Where was the other party?"*

OG: *"Lacey Kingman's abode of habitation. A sugary coming-of-automotivity party."*

You: *"Huh?"*

OG: *"Sweet sixteen."*

You: *"What was it like?"*

OG: *"Very waaaaay. Verrr-ry. A lot of the same revelers but the muncholinos tonight are mucho mucho magnifico."*

You: *"Knowing the way Mike eats, that doesn't surprise me. How do you know Mike?"*

OG: *"Actually, it's his sibling of the female persuasion I am privileged to know. We were in the Convent of Our Lady of Parallel Parking together."*

You: *"Huh?"*

OG: *"Driver's Ed, my man."*

You: *"I've got to take that next semester. What do they make you do?"*

At this point, you're home free. You'll get a blow-by-blow description of Driver's Ed. Like it or not.

When meeting people your age, there are a million things you can ask questions about: schools, teachers, classes, interests,

hobbies, current events, sports, movies, TV shows, travel, music, the Internet, people you know in common. Be alert to visual clues. You can ask someone wearing a Lakers cap about basketball, or someone with lift tickets dangling from his or her parka about skiing.

Now that you know the basics, here are a few conversation fine points:

REMEMBER THAT GOOD CONVERSATION IS AN ART, NOT A SCIENCE.
Keeping a conversation going is kind of like driving a car. You don't just aim and floor it. You have to make constant adjustments in response to the route and driving conditions. The same holds true when you're chattering away. Be alert to body language and verbal cues. You may discover that certain topics go nowhere. If that happens, slam on the brakes and try something new. Or, if someone really starts to bubble with enthusiasm, put your pedal to the metal.

STAY AWAY FROM GOSSIP AND RUMORS.
When you dish dirt, you get covered in it yourself. People think, "Gee, if she says such mean things behind so-and-so's back, how do I know she won't do the same to me?" Backbiting can also get you into some very awkward positions.

Watch how easily this can happen:

You: *"Great party, Tim."*

Tim *"Thanks."*

You: *"Hey, isn't that Jill Banks? Man, I can't believe she actually found your place. I mean, the directions you gave,*

*you had to know left from right. I guess in this age of
diversity, every party has to have a moron. I'm kind
of surprised you invited her."*

Tim: *"I didn't."*

You: *"You mean she just crashed?"*

Tim: *"No. She lives here. She's my stepsister."*

Oops.

DON'T BE NOSY. You'd like to ask a question, but you're not
sure if it's too personal. How can you tell? Ask yourself
how you would feel if someone asked *you* that question—
and everyone in the room could hear your answer. If you'd
feel comfortable, chances are that the question's okay.

In our culture, certain topics are considered off-limits by
many people. ***Examples:*** You wouldn't ask someone you've
just met about their religion or sexuality, or how much
money they make, or if they've had cosmetic surgery.

It's also a good idea to avoid questions that have an
implied judgment or criticism. Like:

"How can you drive such a gas guzzler?"

"Don't you think it's wrong to go out with Jeffrey after
telling Brad you'd go steady with him?"

Although these are reasonable questions for your little
gray cells to ponder, it's bad manners to ask them. Of
course, the rules change if you're talking to a friend. Close
relationships allow for more confiding and challenging—
but you still should be kind and respectful.

DON'T DRINK ALCOHOL. Nothing ruins a good conversation faster or more permanently. Getting drunk is one of the rudest things you can do to your host or social companions. One must stay sober in order to follow the...

4 Simple Rules of Courteous Conversation

1. Don't make speeches.

2. Don't say hurtful things.

3. Don't reveal secrets.

4. Be very, very careful when discussing controversial social, political, moral, and religious issues about which people have strongly held (and often irrational) views.

Polite Listening

Has this ever happened to you? You're talking away, only to realize that your so-called "listener" isn't paying any attention to what you're saying. You might as well be addressing a lamppost. And very few people enjoy talking to lampposts.

Courteous conversationalists use many techniques to show that they're paying attention. Like what? Well, think of everything you could do if someone (like a parent or a teacher) gave you a Big Lecture: You could slouch, sigh, roll your eyeballs, stare at the ceiling, doodle, tap your foot, drum your fingers, shift your position, and/or check your watch. This is known as Communicating Total Indifference.

Polite listeners do the opposite. They:

- sit or stand erect

- look the speaker in the eye

- avoid tapping, squirming, or fidgeting

- grunt, nod, lean forward, smile, frown, raise their eyebrows, and show in other ways that they're paying attention

Plus they cheer people on with such expressions as:

"Hmmm."   "No kidding?"   "Wow!"   "And then?"

"Cool!"   "No way!"   "Really?"

These attitudes, gestures, and responses show that you're hearing what the person is saying. But that's only part of courteous listening. You also want to show that you *understand,* that you actually *care.* You do this by pretending you're a mirror and reflecting the speaker's words back to him or her.

In "lite" talk, it's best to reflect the *informational* content of the speaker's words:

Lou: *Nice weather we're having."*

You: *"It's great to have some sun after all that rain."*

Lou: *"I'm not used to so much rain. I've been living in the Sahara."*

You: *"Wow! You lived in the desert? What was that like?"*

You show Lou that you're listening by making comments and asking questions related to what he's saying. If you respond to "Nice weather we're having" with "I prefer jelly donuts myself," Lou will assume that you haven't been listening (and that you have jelly for brains).

In "heavy" talk, it's best to reflect the *emotional* content of the speaker's words:

Sue: *"I HATE rain. The worst things in my life all happened on rainy days."*

You: *"Rain reminds you of a lot of bad memories?"*

Sue: *"My dog died. My goldfish died. My turtle died. My baby-sitter died. My uncle died."*

You: *"Oh dear. Rain must bring back a lot of sadness."*

You pick up on the fact that Sue isn't really talking about the weather, but about some powerful associations she has with rain. You prove that you're listening by reflecting the feelings behind her words. Your show of empathy will keep Sue talking. She'll sense your support and understanding and will feel safe about revealing herself.

You can see how inappropriate it would be to reply to Sue's statement as if it really were about the weather:

Sue: *"I HATE rain. The worst things in my life all happened on rainy days."*

You: *"I don't mind the rain. But my great-grandfather was a duck—quack, quack."*

When you clue in to what a speaker is saying and respond accordingly, you're using "active listening." This simple strategy says, "I hear you, I understand how you feel, and I accept your right to have those feelings."

 **Is it rude to listen in on other people's conversations if they don't know you're doing it?**

Yes. And no.

Yes if the other people believe that they're speaking without being overheard. This is called *snooping*, and it's a gross invasion of privacy.

No if it's impossible *not* to hear a conversation. Like when the couple at the next table is having an argument, or two kids on a bus are swapping the latest gossip, or some guy in a store is blabbing away on a cell phone. This is called *eavesdropping,* and it's how one learns about life and gathers material for a novel.

Polite eavesdroppers make sure that their presence is known. ***Example:*** If your parents are having a private conversation in the kitchen, they may not realize that you're in the family room and can hear every word they say. Clear your throat or bump a chair. You may lose your chance to eavesdrop, but at least you won't be a little snoop. ◆

Corrections and Interruptions

What do you do when you're talking with someone and she says something you know is wrong? You can think, "You blithering idiot! How can you be so stupid?" But you can't *say* it. Similarly, you can think, "You clumsy oaf!" to the person who steps on your toe and immediately apologizes, but what you should *say* is, "That's all right. No harm done."

Etiquette doesn't ask you to censor your thoughts. It asks you not to say them out loud. It's rude to correct or contradict someone in public—especially an adult. (And adults need to realize that it's also rude to treat children this way.)

Most of the errors people make in conversation just don't matter all that much. They are slips of the tongue, trivial errors of fact, or minor mistakes of pronunciation or grammar. Someone may say "Alan Burr" instead of "Aaron," or get a date wrong, or confuse one event with another. Big whup. It's not worth correcting. And if the person is seriously wrong about something important, chances are her mind is closed to enlightenment. So it's usually best to let it go unless doing so will cause harm.

If you feel that you must issue a correction, here are some guidelines:

DO IT IN PRIVATE. Spare the person from embarrassment by making sure that no audience is present.

DO IT WITH MODESTY. Act as if *you* might be the one who made the mistake. You might say:

> "Isn't that interesting. I was taught that George Washington was the father of our country. But maybe it was George Clooney. Now you've got me curious. I'll have to look it up."

Often, if you're gentle and respectful, the other person will reply:

> "You know, now that you mention it, I think you may be right."

Siblings and close friends who disagree may simply say—

"Is."   "Is."   "Is."

"Is not."   "Is not."   "Is not."

—for however long it takes until one of them gets tired and gives up.

Now, what do you do when you're talking with someone and a third person interrupts you? You can think, "Shut up! Can't you see I'm talking with someone else? What's WRONG with you?" But (you know this already) you can't *say* it. Here's what you *can* do:

1. **Just keep talking.** This is the equivalent of ignoring the rudeness. It can be a lot of fun, because you won't believe how hard it is to keep it up. You're trying to talk, the person you're talking with is trying to talk, and meanwhile, the interrupter blabs on and on. It's

madness! Sometimes, the interrupter will get the point and zip her lip. Usually, she won't. So you'll end up giving in and letting her talk. Any spectators will be very aware of her rudeness and your graciousness in allowing the interruption.

2. **Confront the interrupter.** Turn to her and say, "Just let me get out this one last thought," or, "Please, let me finish what I was saying." Then turn back to the person you were talking with originally.

3. **Speak to the interrupter.** Do it in private. Do it with modesty. Act as if her interrupting is somehow *your* problem. Like this:

> "Ashley, I'm sure you're not aware of this, but sometimes you interrupt me when I'm talking. I'd really appreciate it if you could try not to. I'm such a scatterbrain at times that I need all the help I can get remembering what I want to say."

Don't be a buttinski yourself. If two people are having a conversation and you need to say something to one of them, stand a few feet away and wait. Wait for a pause. Or wait for one of them to turn to you. Then say "Excuse me" and whatever else you need to say.

What if they act as if you're not even there? Maybe they're being rude. Or maybe they're so involved in their conversation that they really aren't aware of your presence. Wander off and try again later. Or you could say something like this:

> "Forgive me for interrupting, but the fireman says we should use the west stairs because the east ones are blocked by a solid

wall of flame. Do you want me to tell you where the exit is, or do you think you can find it on your own?"

Then start to leave. Chances are, they'll pause to get the information you're offering.

 **I have a friend who stutters. If I know what he means to say, is it okay to finish a sentence for him?**

No. In polite conversation, you wait for the other person to finish before speaking. In this case, you simply have to wait a little longer. ◆

Bagging the Bragging

You're a person of many accomplishments, and you're right to think that everyone should know all about them. You may think that the best way to spread the news is to do it yourself.

Don't! Tooting one's own horn is never good form. It's much better to let your actions speak for themselves. There's no need to tell the world about your great save in the game or the prize you won at assembly. Other people were there. They saw it. And if it's something that didn't happen in public, there's another way for word to get out—friends.

Yes, that's what friends are for. Any friend worth his salt will say, "Did you hear? Bilbo bagged the bantamweight belt!" Any friend really worth his salt will say it ten times fast.

When people offer their hearty congratulations, cover yourself with modesty:

"I was so lucky."
"The others deserved it just as much as I did."

You do this because people who say, "Aw, shucks," are much more attractive than those who say, "Ain't I grand!"

How do your friends find out about your successes? You tell them—in a way that reveals your surprise and humble appreciation:

"Guess what? You know that essay contest I entered? I won! I can't believe it!"

This isn't bragging (a form of conceit). It's sharing the joy (a form of giving). Your close friends and family deserve as much.

How to End a Conversation

Now that you know how to get into a conversation and handle some of the fine points and rough spots, you need to know how to get out of one gracefully. This comes in handy when you need to talk to someone else, attend to a personal matter, or escape the awful clutches of the world's greatest bore.

There are several ways to do this. ***Examples:***

1. **The Fake-out.** You could point to a distant spot in the room and say, "Isn't that Tiger Woods?" When the person goes to look, you disappear. By the time he or she turns back, you're long gone.

2. **The Sneak-away.** If a very large person walks between you, you could use him or her for cover, in much the same way that cowboys used to ride out of town hidden behind the flanks of a horse.

Unfortunately, these two techniques are rude, rude, rude. In contrast, the following two are not, so try them first:

1. **The Hand-off.** In one-on-one conversations at a social event, it's impolite to simply walk away from someone, even if there's a pause in the conversation. But it's permissible to make her someone else's problem, er, conversation partner. You do this by saying something like this:

> "Oh, you just have to meet Clarence Darrow."

Approach Clarence, make a proper introduction, give a good clue or two to get the new conversation started ("Clarence has just taken on a new case you may have read about"), then excuse yourself and leave. Clarence may never speak to you again, but at least you're free.

2. **The "Please-Excuse-Me" Ploy.** It's okay to abandon someone as long as you offer an excuse. The ideal excuse leaves the impression that, if it weren't for fate

or duty, you'd happily spend the rest of your life talking to the person. Here are some tried-and-true excuse-mes:

"Please excuse me, but...
...I have to catch Henry before he leaves."
...my ride is about to leave."
...I have to make a call." (This is preferable to "I have to go pee.")

Choose your excuse carefully, because you must follow it through (or at least give the appearance of doing so). It would hurt someone's feelings if you said you had to leave and then hung around the party for another two hours.

If you're on the receiving end of an excuse, take it at face value. **Example:** If someone says, "Excuse me, I'm going to step outside for some fresh air," don't say "Good idea. I think I'll join you." If he wanted your company, he'd say, "Would you like to come outside for some fresh air?"

You can duck out of group conversations a lot more easily. Since the discussion will continue without you (although at nowhere near its former sparkle), you can just say "Excuse me" and depart. This form of "Excuse me" means, "I wouldn't dream of interrupting, so you people just carry on without me."

SPOTLIGHT ON...

MOTORMOUTHS

How do you get out of a conversation with someone who never comes up for air or pauses even for a second so you can say something but instead just keeps talking in an endless stream of words that quickly lose all meaning and your eyes glaze over and your breathing slows and your whole head goes numb and you start having elaborate escape fantasies and dreams of a thousand violent deaths for the motormouth?

If you can't find an opening, you'll have to make one. Come up with an excuse (your bus is about to leave; you have to go help in the kitchen; you have to get to a shop before it closes; etc.). Look surprised, as if you suddenly remembered something important. Place your hand gently on the person's hand (not on his mouth or around his throat). Say:

"I hate to interrupt because I do so enjoy our conversations, but I just remembered that I promised my mother that I'd be home by four."

Then turn and walk away.

What if he follows you, still talking? This is such an outrageous breach of etiquette that you have only one choice: Run like the wind!!!

The Etiquette
of Friendship

Adults often describe the teenage years as the "best years of your life." But teenagers know better. That's because they're smack in the middle of the worry, cruelty, and competition. The pressures and responsibilities. The fears and confusions. The humiliations and torments. The jealousies and rivalries. The hopes and hurt feelings. Adults just have their faded, wrinkled memories.

The greatest pleasures of adolescence are usually linked to one's social life. So are the greatest pains. A lot of the aches and embarrassments could be eliminated if teenagers behaved politely toward one another.

"Yeah, right."

I beg your pardon?

"Teenagers treating each other politely? What planet are YOU from?"

It's true that many teens think that the best way to avoid getting hurt is to get the first punch in. They don't want to be teased, taunted, badmouthed, and shunned, so they tease, taunt, badmouth, and shun others.

Teenagers who use good manners with their peers can dodge much of the suffering and anxiety common during these years. And they will enjoy closer and more rewarding relationships with their friends and romantic interests.

Let's look at some of the ways you can put politeness to work with your peers. But first:

I get teased a lot for having good manners, even by my friends. Why is it considered bad to be polite?

There are still a few bugs to work out in teenage human software. One is the tendency to put people down for being smart, well-behaved, hard-working, and moral.

If you disrespect those traits in others, you don't have to feel bad about not having them yourself.

Don't ever apologize for being polite, principled, responsible, or virtuous. Those very friends who tease you now will discover later on how valuable those qualities are. While they play catch-up, you'll be sitting pretty. ◆

Making New Friends

Is there a proper way to make new friends? Yes: *Act as if you already have as many as you need.*

This may seem like strange advice. But, for some reason, teens are turned off by people who seem desperate to have friends. Maybe they figure that if you want to be friends with *them*, there must be something wrong with *you*. (That's what low self-esteem does for people.)

So do your best to radiate confidence. Be relaxed, yet respectful. Cool, but without an attitude. Eager without sucking up. Mysterious but not stand-offish. Smile enough to show you're at peace, but don't grin like a monkey. Strike a balance. Adjust your aura. Then begin your friends-making campaign.

1. **Observe.** Get a sense of who's who. Check out the pecking orders and groups (jocks, troublemakers, burnouts, wannabes, artists, school leaders, middle-of-the-road good kids, etc.). This will give you some idea of people you'll want to steer clear of and people you'll want to approach.

2. **Inquire.** In a low-key way, ask questions. These can be general ("How do you think the teacher wants us to do these papers?") or personal ("What sport did you letter in?"). Since most teenagers find themselves interesting, they appreciate anyone who asks them questions.

3. **Compliment.** If someone says something noteworthy in class, wears a nice outfit, or makes a good play, tell him so. We all like to be around those who recognize our fine qualities.

4. **Join.** Go out for the team, audition for the band, sign up for the school paper, or get involved with the service club. Being with people who share your interests is one of the best ways to find new friends.

5. **Resist.** You may be approached by teens who are looking for new partners in crime. These are the kids who'll be your friends if you'll be mean to the people they pick on, or if you'll do drugs or cut school with them. These are friends you can do without.

6. **Nurture.** Friendships require time to develop and work to maintain. Once you find a new friend, give her your support, encouragement, loyalty, and empathy. These are things we all want and need.

SPOTLIGHT ON...
TEASING

Is teasing rude? It depends.

It's usually okay to tease people about their positive attributes—looks, accomplishments, popularity, etc. This form of teasing, if done with a light, affectionate touch, is usually meant and taken as a compliment.

It's never okay to tease people about parts of their appearance, background, or behavior that they can't help and/or feel self-conscious about—an accent or stutter, poor grades, a parent in prison, etc.

How do you know whether someone is pleased or embarrassed to have attention drawn to certain talents or features—for example, good grades or a British accent? You just know. Teenagers are highly skilled at detecting the sensitive spots of others.

Coping with Cliques

You may think (and you may be right) that cliques are the height of rudeness. It's fine if people want to be with their friends. There's nothing wrong with that. But do they really have to treat everyone else like dirt?

Of course they don't—and they shouldn't. But knowing that won't make them stop. So what are your choices when faced with (or shut out by) a clique?

YOU CAN START BY UNDERSTANDING WHY SOME PEOPLE FORM CLIQUES. Many teenagers are unsure of themselves socially. They lack self-confidence and social skills. Cliques and gangs (which are really just cliques carried to an extreme) give them love, approval, protection, and support. The more a clique's members put other people down, the cooler they think they are.

YOU CAN DECIDE WHETHER BELONGING TO A PARTICULAR CLIQUE IS REALLY THAT IMPORTANT TO YOU. What, if anything, do they have that you want? When you closely examine a particular clique, you may find that they're not as special or elite as they'd like you to believe.

IF YOU'RE CONVINCED THAT YOUR LIFE WILL BE MEANINGLESS AND EMPTY IF YOU'RE NOT PART OF A CERTAIN CLIQUE, THEN DO WHAT YOU CAN TO JOIN. You can try making friends with one member. (**TIP:** Approach the person when he or she isn't surrounded by other members. Your chances of being scorned and rejected will be somewhat reduced.) Maybe you have interests in common. Once you've established that friendship, you may find that you're automatically part of the clique. (And once you're in, you can try to influence the clique to stop being so nasty to outsiders.)

Of course, you have another alternative:

YOU CAN IGNORE THE CLIQUE. Follow the steps in "Making New Friends" on page 40. Find other people who are warm, interesting, inviting, and open-minded. The chances are excellent that they'll welcome you and return your friendship.

Friends with Disabilities

One of the greatest challenges that people with disabilities (PWDs) face is dealing with the manners-impaired. These "well-meaning" folks talk about a disabled person as if she's not there or can't hear:

> "Can she walk?"
> "Will she grow?"
> "Isn't she brave!!!"

They pry into areas that are none of their business:

> "Were you born that way?"
> "Can you have sex?"
> "Do you think you'll ever have children?"

They treat the person as an object of pity or praise, not as a human being with needs and feelings no different than their own.

Many people feel uncomfortable around PWDs because they don't know how to act—or react. Or they may not know how or whether to help. Or they may view a disability through their own perspective. Maybe you can't imagine what it would be like to be blind, or deaf, or unable to walk. Just thinking about it is scary. Your fear will affect how you act toward and around PWDs.

The essence of good manners is the ability to put others at ease regardless of one's own discomfort. In other words, get over yourself. Don't miss out on the chance to turn PWDs into FWDs (Friends with Disabilities). All it takes is a little awareness, some common sense, and these helpful do's and taboos:

DON'T ASSUME THAT ONE DISABILITY IMPLIES ANOTHER. There's no need to shout at a blind person or speak s-l-o-w-l-y to someone in a wheelchair.

ALWAYS ADDRESS PWDS DIRECTLY. Look them in the eye. Just because they may have a parent, friend, or nurse with them doesn't mean they can't speak for themselves. Never refer to them in the third person in their presence ("Would he mind if I took him for a walk?" "Can she swim?").

WHEN TALKING TO A PERSON WHO IS DEAF, FACE HIM SO HE CAN READ YOUR LIPS. If an interpreter is present, face the person who is hearing impaired, not the interpreter.

WHEN WALKING WITH A PERSON WHO IS BLIND, DON'T PULL HER BY THE HAND OR STEER HER BY THE SHOULDERS. Offer her your elbow. If she chooses to take it, let her set the pace. If you approach an obstacle or hazard, don't just shout, "Look out!" Instead, give her specific information: "First, there's a big mound of dog doo-doo. Second, there are four really steep steps."

WHEN SPEAKING TO WHEELCHAIR USERS, TRY TO POSITION YOURSELF AT THEIR EYE LEVEL. Sit down and face them, or, if you're standing, bend at the waist. But don't squat or kneel. This might seem condescending.

BE PATIENT WHEN TALKING WITH PEOPLE WHO HAVE A SPEECH DISORDER. Don't finish their sentences for them. Don't pretend that you understand what they're saying if you really don't. Say, "I'm sorry, I didn't get that," or, "You went where?" or, "What was that number again?"

ALWAYS ASK BEFORE HELPING. If you saw someone struggling to carry a lot of luggage, you wouldn't just grab the bags out of her hands. You'd ask if she could use some assistance. The same thing applies to PWDs. Don't start steering them across the hall, down the aisle, or across the street as if they were grocery carts. Say, "Would you like to take my arm?" or, "May I help in any way?" They will either say, "Yes, please," or, "No, thanks."

DON'T PRY. PWDs don't owe anyone a medical report. It's rude to ask about the causes, symptoms, past, future, or limitations of their condition.

HELP TO RAISE OTHER PEOPLE'S AWARENESS AND SENSITIVITY TO PWDS. *Example:* If you're out and about with your FWDs, other people (such as waiters, sales clerks, or acquaintances of yours) might address you rather than your friends. If this happens, don't respond or make eye contact. This will encourage them to speak directly to your friends.

NEVER TOUCH A PWD WITHOUT PERMISSION. This is an invasion of his or her personal space. (So is leaning on a wheelchair.)

NEVER PET OR CALL TO A SERVICE ANIMAL, SUCH AS A GUIDE DOG, WITHOUT THE OWNER'S PERMISSION. This could distract the animal and/or interfere with its training.

DON'T USE EUPHEMISMS TO DESCRIBE DISABILITIES. Disability groups object to terms such as "handicapable," "mentally different," "physically inconvenienced," and "physically challenged." These terms reinforce the idea that disabilities can't be dealt with up front.

USE RESPECTFUL LANGUAGE. Would you like it if someone called you a cripple, a feeb, or a spastic? Then don't use those words to talk about someone who's physically disabled, has mental retardation, or has a motor disorder.

DON'T DEFINE PEOPLE BY THEIR DISABILITIES. If you need to mention the disability, always put the person first, not the disability. *Example:* Say "Arnie, my friend who is blind," not "My blind friend Arnie."

DON'T WORRY ABOUT USING THE "WRONG" WORDS BY MISTAKE. A blind person won't be offended if you say, "See what I mean?" or, "I hear the math sub is tough. You better watch out for her!" A person who is physically disabled won't take it wrong if you say, "Later—gotta run!" But do avoid the all-too-common expressions that use disabilities as insults. ***Examples:*** Don't say, "What's the matter, are you blind?!?" to a person who steps on your toe. Or shout, "You retard!" to someone who makes a mistake.

If You're a PWD...

You've probably dealt with plenty of clueless people. You can't change the world, but you can set a good example and hope that others will follow.

Treat others the way you'd like them to treat you. Introduce yourself in social situations. Practice the fine art of conversation, which mostly involves getting people to talk about themselves. Ignore comments and whispers—and don't assume they're always about you.

You're not responsible for the social disabilities of others. You don't owe anybody an explanation of why you are the way you are, or what "happened" to you. If you want to speak out, that's fine. But it's not your job to satisfy people's curiosity, and you have a right to your privacy.

What about the lout who insists on knowing what's "wrong" with you? Simply asking that question is rude, *rude,* RUDE. Should you be rude back? No...but by all means, make him squirm. Slowly turn your head toward him. Give him a hard look a nanosecond short of a stare. Then slowly look away.

Or smile and say, "There's nothing wrong with me. Is there something wrong with you?"

Or smile and say, "Do you think the Orioles will win the pennant?"

Or smile and say, "I'm sorry, but I don't discuss such things with people I don't know."

Some people may ask about your disability because they want to get to know you better. (As opposed to those who are just being nosy.) You'll probably sense when a question indicates sincere interest, and you'll feel more comfortable answering it. Or not. Either way, it's your choice.

I use a wheelchair. How can I stop people from helping me?

Most people would never dream of picking up complete strangers and carrying them across the street. Yet they think it's perfectly fine to start pushing someone's wheelchair!

You might tell these eager beavers, "Thank you, but I don't need any assistance." And then, if you feel like it, do a few 360s, pop a wheelie or two, and scorch on outta there. ◆

Handling Friendship Problems Politely

No relationship is 100 percent problem-free. That's because people are imperfect creatures. They make mistakes, act selfishly, change their minds, have their own ideas and beliefs, and sometimes get up on the wrong side of the bed. Here's what to do during rough times in your friendships.

Peer Pressure

What if you learn that the people you hang out with do things that are questionable, or even against the law? How can you avoid getting involved without seeming stuck-up or rude?

Just say no.

"But, the 'Just Say No' campaign didn't work!"

True...but that's because they didn't say, "No, thank you."
Saying no is the ultimate act of personal control. When you're pressured to do something you don't want to do, simply respond with one of these phrases:

"No, thank you."　　　　　　**"I can't."**

　　"I'd rather not."　　　　　**"I don't want to."**

Beyond that, you don't owe anyone an explanation.
With certain people, in certain situations, you may wish to provide an explanation out of respect or to prevent more problems. ***Examples:***

- You've been seriously dating someone for quite a while. She recently told you that she wants to have sex. If you just say no, she might wonder if there's something wrong with her, or if you're seeing someone else, or if you don't really like her—all kinds of things that aren't your real reason. So you might want to say something like, "I care about you a lot, and I want us to keep seeing each other, but I don't want to have sex with anyone yet." Or perhaps something like, "I care about you a lot, and I want us to keep seeing each other, but I have lice."

- You've just been invited to join some of your friends for a late-night activity. Their plan is to spray-paint graffiti on the walls of your school. If you just say no, they'll go ahead and do it without you. So you might want to say something like, "Ha, ha, you guys are so full of it. I know you can't be serious. If you get caught, you'll be expelled. Even if you don't get caught, a lot of people will be angry and hurt. Why don't we shoot hoops instead, or see that new movie at the multiplex?"

Whatever the circumstances, stand firm. Nobody can make you do anything you don't want to do. And you may discover that the minute one brave soul (namely you) says no, others will follow.

Getting High

Being an intelligent, sensible person, you've already decided not to use drugs. But some of your friends keep asking you to get high with them anyway. What's the polite thing to say?

It's nice that your friends have learned to share. But that's not the issue here. When someone offers you something you don't want—whether it's a joint or a jelly sandwich—simply say, "No, thank you."

If the person who's inviting you to get high has good manners, that's all you'll have to say. But since that's not very likely, here's how to respond when he or she persists:

Stoner friend: *"Wanna get high?"*

You: *"No, thank you."*

SF: *"Why not?"*

You: *"I'd prefer not to, thank you."*

SF: *"Whatsa matter, ya scared?"*

You: *"I'd prefer not to, thank you."*

SF: *"Oh, come on."*

You: *"I'd prefer not to, thank you."*

SF: *"It's not gonna kill ya."*

You: *"I'd prefer not to, thank you."*

SF: *"Just try it."*

You: *"I'd prefer not to, thank you."*

SF: *"Oh, forget it!"*

Just remember that you don't owe anybody an explanation for your decision. In fact, it's rude of the person to ask. Responding to such pressure just prolongs the discussion and puts you on the defensive. See what happens if you try to answer the questions:

SF: *"Wanna get high?"*

You: *"No, thank you."*

SF: *"Why not?"*

You: *"Because I don't want to take drugs."*

SF: *"Whatsa matter, ya scared?"*

You: *"No, I'm not scared."*

SF: *"Then what?"*

You: *"I just don't want to."*

SF: *"Have you ever tried it?"*

You: *"No."*

SF: *"Then how do you know?"*
You: *"I've never jumped off a cliff, but I know I don't want to."*
SF: *"That's different. Jumping off a cliff could kill you."*
You: *"So could drugs."*
SF: *"How do you know? You think you know everything?"*
You: *"I didn't say that."*

And so on.

If you stand firm and don't get into a debate, you'll wear the other person down. This strategy can be used to refuse almost any invitation:

> "I'm sorry, but I'd prefer not to shoplift, thank you."
>
> "I'm just not able to smash mailboxes, but thank you for asking."

As a matter of etiquette, it's not your responsibility to make judgments or point out dangers associated with those behaviors. As a matter of friendship, it may be. Real friends don't let other friends do stupid, dangerous, illegal things. Like...

Drinking and Driving

You and your friend go together to a party. He drives. Alcohol is available, and your friend spends most of the night hanging around the rum punch. As the party comes to an end, he grabs his coat, fumbles for his keys, and says, "Lesh go, hokay?"

He's so far out of his gourd that he doesn't know which end is up. He's about to turn 4,000 pounds of steel into a lethal weapon, and he expects *you* to sit in the passenger seat!

Since you haven't been drinking, you still have your good manners, your common sense, and your survival instincts. So you respond with one of the following:

"Please don't leave. We would all miss you terribly. I'll talk to the host. I'm sure he'll want you to spend the night here."

"You really don't look well. Come with me. I'll show you where you can lie down."

"I know you think I'm crazy, but I could never forgive myself if I let you drive and something happened. Just let me have my way, okay? Stay around."

"Amy says she'll take you home. We'll help you get your car tomorrow. I'll get a ride with Peter."

"Hand me your keys, please. I'm calling a cab."

Or, if you're a licensed driver:

"Hand me your keys, please. I'll drive you home and return your car to you first thing tomorrow morning."

If none of these approaches works, gather several of your largest friends. Then sit on the person and pry the keys out of his fingers.

This is not impolite. Etiquette allows a lot of leeway when it comes to saving lives. For example, shoving a total stranger would be considered bad manners in normal circumstances. Doing so to move him out of the path of an oncoming bus would be heroic.

So don't worry about being seen as rude for not letting a friend drive drunk. It's likely the person won't even remember what you said or did. And if he gives you a hard time the next day, simply say:

> "Your friendship and safety are so important to me that I'm happy to put up with your anger. And I'll do it again if it will keep you from killing yourself or others."

Backbiting

You've just heard that one of your friends has been saying mean things about you behind your back. Naturally, you're hurt and upset. Should you say something or drop him?

That depends.

You have only the word of the person who told you—who spoke behind the back of the friend who allegedly spoke behind *your* back. But where did Person B (the tattler) get the news about Person A (your friend)? Did he hear it directly from your friend (A)? Or from someone else (C) who heard it from someone else (D) who heard it from someone else (E) who heard it from your friend (A)?

In other words, how many people were involved in passing this information along to you?

It's best not to take this kind of communication too seriously. You have no idea what your friend really said. To put this another way, imagine that he bakes a big plate of brownies as a gift for you. He hands the plate to a friend and says, "Please give these to Jeff." The friend figures no one will miss one brownie, so he takes one and hands the plate to another friend with instructions to "Give this to Jeff." The plate goes through 12 more people, and each takes a brownie, rearranges the rest, and passes it on. By the time it gets to you, there's just a bunch of crumbs. And you think, "What kind of a lousy cheap present is this?"

Now watch what happens when words instead of brownies get passed along:

Andy to Sandy: *"I'm worried about Jeff. His parents are getting a divorce, and he seems pretty upset. I wish there was something I could do to help."*

Sandy to Mandy: *"Andy's really upset that Jeff's parents are divorcing. He wishes he could do something to help Jeff."*

Mandy to Randy: *"Andy said that Jeff's parents are really upset about getting divorced. Apparently Jeff's been getting some kind of help."*

Randy to Candy: *"According to Andy, Jeff's parents are getting divorced because Jeff is in some kind of trouble and needs a lot of help."*

And this is what finally reaches you:

Candy: *"Andy's been telling people that it's all your fault that your parents are getting divorced and that you're going to have to go to this special school that helps kids who are in trouble."*

The only way to check out the backbiting rumor is to talk to your friend. He probably said *something*. But there may have been another part of the conversation that didn't get passed along. Give him the benefit of the doubt. Tell him what you heard and how it made you feel:

"I can't believe that *you'd* say something like that, *so* I wanted to ask *you* about it."

You may find that the whole thing was just a misunderstanding. Or you may learn that your friend is guilty as charged. In that case, you'll have to decide if and/or how things can be patched up.

Shunning

One day, for no apparent reason, your friends start acting like jerks. They don't return your calls, they don't IM you, and when you see them in school, they don't stop to talk. You know they're getting together without you. What's up…and what can you do?

It can feel very lonely and weird when people you like and trust suddenly give you the cold shoulder. If *one* friend does this, maybe he *is* a jerk and you should just write him off. But if you're having problems with *all* of your friends, it may be because of something *you* did (or they mistakenly think you did).

Take a close look at yourself. Has your behavior changed? Have you been upset, negative, or cranky? Have you said or done anything that might have hurt or offended someone? Even if your friends are behaving badly toward you—even if they're being selfish, snooty, or petty—stop and think about your own words and actions. Keep in mind that you can't control your friends; you can only control *yourself*. The way to get other people to change their behavior is to change your own. This works with friends, parents, teachers, bosses—anybody.

If you can't think of any reasons for the way your friends are treating you, seek out the one friend you trust the most. Approach her when she isn't with the rest of the group and doesn't have to put up a front. Tell her that you value her friendship, but you've noticed that she and the others don't seem to want you around lately. Explain that this has upset you, and you wonder if you've done something wrong. She may give you some feedback that will point the way to changes you can make, or reveal a misunderstanding that you can set straight.

It's also possible that you're simply yesterday's friend. Sad but true, relationships among teenagers can be fickle, painful, and short-lived. Friends drop friends for reasons both good and lousy. If this particular group has decided to reject you, you can't force them to take you back. But you can hold your head high and make new friends. If your old group later decides that they want you back, you can choose to resume those friendships or not. But whatever you do, don't drop your new friends. You know how much that can hurt.

SPOTLIGHT ON...
APOLOGIZING

You did something terrible to one of your friends. Maybe you spread a rumor, told a lie, or hurt her feelings on purpose. You've been avoiding each other ever since, but you want her back as a friend. What should you do?

Apologize, apologize, apologize. Say you're sorry and really mean it.

You can do this in person (if she's willing to talk to you), or by writing a note. Don't beat around the bush. Admit what you did. Don't make excuses, or say that it was no big deal, or blame your friend for being "too sensitive" or unable to "take a joke." Take full responsibility for what you did, and make it clear that you're totally, miserably sorry.

Say that the last thing you'd ever want to do would be to hurt or embarrass a friend. Say that you don't know how you could have been so careless, thoughtless, and rude. Say you can understand if she never wants to see you again, and that you'd give anything to turn back the clock. Say that you know you don't deserve it, but you hope she'll be able to forgive you.

If your friendship is strong, she *will* forgive you. After hearing how sad and guilty you've been feeling, she may even try to comfort you.

Finally, whatever you did, don't ever do it again.

Taking Sides

If you have more than one friend (and let's hope you do), chances are that at some point two of them won't get along. And each will want you to take sides against the other.

Adults face this situation when friends divorce, and each spouse tries to convince his or her friends that it was the other spouse's fault.

It's best to stay out of the crossfire. Friendship doesn't obligate you to enlist every time one of your friends goes to war.

When your friends begin to badmouth each other, hold up a hand and say:

> "Stop! I'm very sorry that you and Meg are angry at each other, and I know how upsetting that must be. But I like you both too much to get caught in the middle or choose sides. I'm sure that if you and Meg sit down and talk about the problem, you can resolve it."

This doesn't mean that you can't use information you learn from one or the other to try to arrange a truce. **Example:** If one of your friends said, "You know, if she'd just apologize, I'd be willing to forget the whole thing," you could mention to the other friend, "You know, I'm sure if you just apologized, Meg would be willing to forget the whole thing."

Blabbing Secrets

Have you ever had a friend (note the past tense—*had*) who couldn't keep a secret? This is one of the most serious and most common of all friendship problems. Keeping secrets is hard, and the temptation to share them is great, because information is power. When someone blabs a secret, they're saying, "I know something you don't know. I'm in the loop and you're not. Nya, nya."

Not all secret-spillers are mean on purpose. In their mind, they're not really breaking a confidence, because they're only telling a friend they know they can trust. Of course, that friend tells *her* best friend, who tells *her* best friend, and before you know it, your secret makes the rounds of the entire school.

There's only one surefire way to keep someone from spilling one of your secrets: Don't tell it in the first place. But if you must tell someone, make sure it's a person who's told *you* a lot of secrets. This is known as *mutual deterrence.* It's what two countries do when they point nuclear weapons at each other. Since either has the power to destroy the other, neither makes the first move.

5 Reasons Why Friends Are Sometimes Mean...

They snoop. They rat. They backbite and shun. They spread stories and rumors. They laugh about your problems. And these are your friends? Why are people so mean?

Maybe they're thoughtless. Some people are sloppy about how they go through life. They don't take the time to think before they speak or act.

Maybe they lack empathy. Some people are self-centered. They don't consider how things look or feel to other people.

Maybe they're intolerant. Children learn intolerance from their parents, political and religious leaders, societal messages, etc. Prejudiced people wouldn't call their behavior "mean." But that's what it is—and worse.

Maybe they believe that the world owes them something. People who feel that life has treated them badly may think they're entitled to take what they want and abuse others. They see this as "getting their fair share," not as being mean.

Maybe they have a lousy self-image. People who hurt others are often in great pain themselves. Putting others down is a power trip that covers up their own insecurities.

Of course, none of these "causes" is an excuse for being mean. But they might help you understand the friend who sometimes treats you badly.

...And 3 Things You Can Do When They Are

What are your choices when a friend is mean?

1. **Drop him.** Life is too short to have mean friends.

2. **Wait and see what happens.** The friendship may dry up and die on its own. It may go back to normal. Your own feelings may change. Your friend may apologize.

3. **Try talking with your friend.** Tell him how you feel about what he did. Don't accuse or attack. Focus on your own shock, embarrassment, and hurt. He may be feeling very sorry, and he'll take this opportunity to apologize.

Dodging Debts

You're a kind and generous person, so you occasionally agree to loan money to a friend. But what should you do when the friend doesn't pay you back? Since dodging a debt is rude, you might say:

> "You know that ten dollars I loaned you last week? I'm sure it's just slipped your mind, but I need it back."

By giving your friend the benefit of the doubt, you offer her a face-saving way out. If she says that she doesn't have the money right now, try to set up a payment plan. Could she give you two dollars a week? You'll quickly learn whether she plans to repay you or string you along. If she's a bad debt, you may have to absorb your loss.

It's wise to see whether friends repay a first loan before you agree to a second (or a third). This way, you cut your losses early. For larger loans (for example, the $50 or $100 a friend needs toward a new pair of track shoes), write a letter stating the amount and outlining a payment schedule. This prevents misunderstandings and keeps the transaction businesslike.

Many friends loan money back and forth to tide each other over during lean times. This is fine, as long as things stay relatively even. If you keep getting the short end of the deal, you may need to cut off the cash flow.

Friends Who Can't Take a Hint

You know the ones. They come to your house and stay forever. They call you on the phone and won't hang up. They find you online and IM you until you want to throw your computer through the window...or turn off your instant messaging, but then your other friends wouldn't be able to reach you!

How can you, without being rude, get hintless ones to leave, hang up, or sign off?

You'll need to be more assertive—and forearmed. When you issue an invitation, include an end time. Say:

"Do you want to come over this afternoon? I have to start my homework at six. But you could stay until then."

For those never-ending phone calls, have a list of excuses handy:

"I have to eat dinner now."

"I need to make another call before it gets too late."

"My dad has to use the phone."

"My mom asked me to help her with something."

For those nonstop IMs, type:

can't sign off cuz waiting to hear bout the math
test from som1 else but going AFK 4 awhile
cya 2morrow in sch%l! BFN

When you offer an excuse, preface it politely. As in:

"I wish you could stay longer, but...."

"I'd love to talk more, but...."

I cd chat 24/7 but....

Jealousy

Sometimes it may seem as if your friends are better than you. Maybe they're winning more prizes, getting better grades, or wearing cooler clothes. Perhaps they're more popular or attractive or smart. Whatever, you wake up one day feeling like a total loser—and jealous besides.

It's hard when other people seem to have all the luck and success, especially when they're your friends. It's natural to feel jealous. But you're overlooking one thing: They have chosen *you* for their friend. Do you think they'd hang out with a total loser? No way. This means there must be something wonderful in you that they see and you don't.

People are successful in all sorts of different ways. Maybe you're a terrific "people person"—considerate, well-mannered, responsible, trustworthy, helpful, empathetic, caring, loyal, supportive, and fun to be with. Those are real talents. They're just not as easy to measure as grades earned or goals scored. You may tell yourself that those things don't count. But they do. In fact, you'll go a lot farther in life, and find a lot more fulfillment, than will people who are great students or athletes but lack those skills.

Being a friend means showing pleasure in your friends' prizes, trophies, and honors—even when you're hurting inside. But that hurt will go away if you take the friendship of these high achievers for the compliment it is. Focus on the strengths and talents you have, rather than the ones you may not have.

When Friends Bring Their Problems and Secrets to You

Do your friends tell you their problems? Is yours the shoulder they lean on and cry on? Do they reveal things to you that they wouldn't tell anyone else in the whole wide world?

On the one hand, this can be a compliment. It means that your friends trust you with their secrets. They know what a good listener you are. They value your advice.

On the other, it can be a drag. What if you don't know what to say? What if you say the wrong things?

Chances are, you're already saying the right things, or you wouldn't have so many friends confiding in you. For everyday problems and normal teenage mood swings, here are some good ways to respond.

True Confessions

JUST LISTEN. Most people, when they have problems, just want somebody to listen. They're feeling alone, abnormal, afraid, or confused. If all you do is listen, you might give your friend 90 percent of what she needs. If you've dealt with a similar problem in your own life, share your experience. If you see a possible solution, suggest it.

ASK QUESTIONS. This is a good way to help people put their troubles in perspective. First, help your friend define the problem. What does she think is wrong? What does she need? How does she feel? Next, help her brainstorm solutions. Which one seems best to her? Which seems most likely to help? Which would she like to try first? Encourage her to come up with a plan of action. Later, follow through by asking how she's doing.

BE SURE NOT TO MINIMIZE THE PROBLEM. When trying to help your friends feel better, you may say things to comfort them that end up making light of their feelings or situation:

"You'll get over it."
"It's not that big a deal."

"You'll get another chance."
"That happens to lots of people."
"It'll be all right."

Of course, these things may all be true. But people who are upset don't want logic or tired old sayings. They want sympathy, love, understanding, and acceptance. They want you to know that they're hurting. To be a real friend, show that you know and give them what they need.

Example: If a friend says that her father has to have an operation for cancer, don't say, "Oh, I'm sure it will turn out fine." Even though you're saying it to cheer her up, you don't know how the operation will turn out. Neither does she, and that's why she's scared to death. Say, "That must be really frightening," or, "I'd be so worried if my father had to have an operation."

OFFER ASSISTANCE. When friends come to you with problems, ask them if there's anything you can do to help. They'll probably say "No." When they do, say, "Okay, but promise you'll tell me if there is. I really want to help." This lets them know you're sincere and they're not alone.

SHOW THAT YOU'RE NOT AFRAID TO TALK ABOUT DIFFICULT THINGS. Sometimes, after sharing a problem, teenagers will feel embarrassed or wish they could take back what they said. The next time you talk to your friend, tell her how glad you were that she told you about her troubles. Then ask her how she's feeling and how it's going. If it's obvious that she doesn't want to talk about it anymore, let it pass.

BE ALERT TO THE POSSIBILITY THAT THERE'S MORE TO THE STORY THAN YOU'RE BEING TOLD. Friends with serious problems will sometimes only tell you the tip of the iceberg. They may be in denial; they may be ashamed; they may be hesitant to spill a family secret.

Examples: Someone says that his parents "aren't getting along," but what's really happening on the home front are knock-down-drag-out fights. Or someone says he's been "experimenting" with drugs, when in fact he's been using them every day for six months.

If you suspect that you're not getting the whole story, you'll need to encourage your friend to say more. If you ask, "Do you want to talk about it?" it's too easy for him to say "No." Instead, try saying, "It sounds like things are pretty rough for you right now. Please tell me what's going on." In your friend's mind, this turns talking into a kindness he can do for you.

 **What are you supposed to say if a friend tells you he's gay?**

That depends on how and why it's said. If it's mentioned in passing ("I'd love to come to your barbecue, but my boyfriend and I are going to the Gay Pride rally that day"), treat it as you would any other piece of information. Say, "We'll miss you," or, "Have a good time!" or, "You'll have to tell me what it was like."

If it's said to set things straight (so to speak), say, "You're very kind to tell me."

If it's said as a proud disclosure of identity, offer the person your best wishes for a life full of much love and happiness.

If it's said in confidence by a friend who's troubled by his sexuality, respond with warmth, support, and empathy. Encourage him to talk. If specific things are upsetting him (for example, how to tell his parents, or harassment at school), help him to explore options for dealing with these issues.

If your school is "gay-friendly," he may find a student support group and/or empathetic counselors. He could also look in local bookstores for some of the excellent books written for gay and lesbian teens. Most larger cities have gay- and lesbian-themed bookstores and newspapers, which are other good sources of information. Support groups for gay and lesbian youth can be found by looking in the Yellow Pages under "Gay Organizations" or "Social and Human Services" or by calling a hotline. Finally, if your friend has access to a computer and the Internet, there are sites on the World Wide Web for, about, and by gay teens.

There's no need for a gay or lesbian teenager to deal with these issues alone. Be a real friend and see that he doesn't have to. ◆

Alarm Bells

Listening, asking questions, and offering help should work for most everyday problems and situations teens face. But what about when you suspect that a friend is being abused at home? When you believe that a friend has an eating disorder or is abusing drugs? What about when a friend says that she's going to kill herself?

These are not problems you should expect—or try—to solve by yourself.

The best thing you can do for a friend who's showing signs of trouble is to tell an adult—your parent, a teacher you trust who knows you both, the school counselor, another adult leader. Describe what you've seen and heard. Say that you're afraid for your friend, and you want the adult to help.

What about the friend who tells you that she's suicidal? She may be confiding in you in the hope (conscious or not) that you'll "force" her to get help. Even if she resists, try to get her to see a counselor, talk to a trusted adult, or contact a hotline. Explain that you're very concerned about her and will do everything you can to help.

If your friend refuses or wants you to swear not to tell, don't back off or let it go. Talk to

your parents or another trusted adult. Tell them what you know about your friend and ask for their help.

It's worth risking the friendship if your friend's life or health are in danger. She may be angry at first. But if she gets the help she needs, she'll eventually think of you as the best friend she ever had. And if she drops you or comes to greater harm, at least you'll know you did everything you could to help.

SPOTLIGHT ON...

TAKING CARE OF #1

It's great if you're someone other people can talk to. That says a lot about the kind of person you are.

Just don't let yourself get weighed down by other people's problems. Don't be a soggy shoulder. Take time to take care of yourself. And make sure that *you* have someone to talk to about *your* problems—someone you trust to listen with respect, care, and empathy.

The strongest, longest-lasting friendships are those where both people can talk—and listen. Both people can ask for comfort and advice—and give it.

The Etiquette
of Romance

During elementary school, most kids' energy goes into the three Rs: TV, video games, and playing with their friends.

"Wait—those don't start with R!"

Neither do writing and arithmetic.

Once junior high rolls around, a fourth R is added, and this one makes sense: *Romance.*

Hormones start humming, and suddenly the world looks very different. Obnoxious boys turn into *cute* obnoxious boys. Giggly girls turn into *cute* giggly girls. The fear of cooties is set aside, the hunt is on, and suddenly you need to learn a new set of social skills: asking someone out, being asked out, and (unless the first person you meet turns out to be your soul mate, which is *very* unlikely), breaking up.

Asking Someone Out

Before you plant, you must prepare the soil. Similar groundwork must be undertaken before asking someone for a date. Here are nine tips that will increase your chances of success:

1. **Get to know the person first.** Most of us are taught never to go anywhere with strangers. So take the time and make the effort to learn about the person you want to ask out. Give him a chance to learn something about you. Talk in class (but not *during* class). Sit together at lunch. Hang out in the same group(s). See if you have things in common and if you enjoy each other's company. If all systems are go...

2. **Ask early.** Give the person advance notice—three to four days for informal dates such as dinner, a movie, or paintball. This allows her plenty of time to check with her parents, earn some extra money, reschedule an appointment, decide what to wear, etc.

   Last-minute invitations are likely to be rejected. Either she has other plans, or she doesn't have other plans and wants to hide the fact, or she assumes (rightly or wrongly) that you couldn't get anyone else to go.

   There is an exception to the ask-early rule: an occasion that couldn't have been anticipated. As in:

"I just found out that my uncle is sailing his boat up tomorrow. Do you want to go out on the bay with us?"

3. **Don't ask too early.** Being overeager doesn't look good, and it makes both people feel silly:

"Would you like to go to the senior prom with me?"

"Gee, I don't know. I'm flattered that you asked. Let's see how we feel about each other in two years."

4. **Choose the right moment.** You know how important timing is when asking your parents for permission to do something. The same holds true for asking someone out on a date. You don't want to pop the question if the person is upset, distracted, surrounded by other people, or rushing madly to class. Wait for a calm, private moment.

5. **Do the asking yourself.** Throughout history, certain individuals have willingly done the dirty work of others. In the adult world, these people are called *lawyers*. In the teenage world, they're called *friends*.

   It's understandable why you might want a friend to ask someone out for you. Rejection (the fifth R) is easier to take if it comes secondhand. Plus, if you don't do the actual inviting, you have what's known as *plausible deniability*. When the rumors of your rejection start to fly, you can say, "What do you mean? I never asked him out."

   Those are the positives of letting your friends do the asking. Here are the negatives:

▓ Secondhand invitations make you look like a wuss. Harsh, but true.

▓ Secondhand invitations promote miscommunication. You can never be sure of who really said what, especially if the answer was no. Was it an "I'll-never-go-out-with-him" no, or "I-might-go-out-with-him-but-not-to-that" no, or "I'd-love-to-go-out-with-him-but-can't-that-night" no? You'll never no, er, know.

▓ Secondhand invitations promote gossip and rumors. If you ask someone out and get turned down, only two people know. If a friend does the asking, it becomes a public matter. By tomorrow morning, the gory details could be all over school.

So resist the temptation to use friends as social secretaries. Issue your invitations face-to-face, phone-to-phone, or in writing.

6. Go s-l-o-w-l-y. Some people (there are three in North America) have no trouble asking for a date. Full of confidence and charm, they pick up the phone, propose a wonderful evening, wait for the yes, and carry out their plans with style and ease.

Most people are a bit less sure of themselves. You know what that can be like. You agonize for weeks or months: "Does she like me? What if I don't have anything to say? What if the answer's no? What if I make a fool of myself? Where would we go?" Finally, you gather enough courage to pop the question. With pounding heart and flip-flopping stomach, you pick up the phone and dial. And slam it down again. After eleven tries, you let it ring. She answers. And in a firm, confident voice, you say "Gulp."

When you ask someone out for the first time, take it easy. Think date with a small *d*. Don't plan a six-hour evening where you'll be all alone in new or stressful circumstances. Do something low-key and informal. Go to a basketball game with a group of friends. Play tennis. Go skating. See a movie. Hang out at the mall. Your comfort and friendship will grow, and you'll know when the time is right to ask for a date with a big *D*.

You may be thinking, "But I'm cool. I can handle anything." That may be true, but your date might not feel the same way. Take things slowly for her—or his—sake.

7. **Be specific.** If you issue a vague invitation, you're asking for it. Not a date—a major bummer. As in:

> "You wanna go out sometime?"
> "No."

Even if the person replies "Sure," she may be thinking, "In a hundred million years." And you have no way of knowing.

Here's the difference between being vague and being specific:

Vague—No!	Specific—Yes!
"What're ya doin' Friday night?"	"Are you free Friday night to go ice-skating?"
"Ya wanna go out with me?"	"Would you like to go to the Halloween Dance with me?"
"How 'bout doin' somethin' sometime?"	"I'm wondering if you'd be interested in seeing that new documentary on bighorn elks at the Rialto. Maybe this Saturday? It's only showing for a week."

Once you've issued the invitation, you can provide further details on time, place, mode of transportation, curfews, special clothing or equipment needed, etc.

8. Be positive. Negative invitations make it easy to say no:

"You wouldn't want to go to the movies with me, would you?" (No, I wouldn't.)

"I don't suppose you're free next Thursday?" (No, I'm not.)

Some people think that negative invitations soften the blow of rejection ("I got turned down, but at least I guessed right!"). But why set up a self-fulling prophecy?

Plus these kinds of invites require the person to contradict you in order to accept. That's too confusing and too much work:

"You wouldn't want to go to the movies with me, would you?" (Well, yes, I would, but if you think I wouldn't, then maybe I shouldn't.)

"I don't suppose you're free next Thursday?" (Actually, I am, but if you think I'm not, then I probably shouldn't be, because what does that say about my social schedule? So I'd better find something else to do.)

Remember that an invitation from you is a compliment. It says, "I and my wonderful self desire your company." Let that be your message. If you still get turned down, at least you gave it your best shot.

9. **Be up-front about money.** Let's say you want to invite someone out, but you don't have enough moola. Or you've been invited to a concert, but the tickets cost $35—too much for you.

Don't let money keep you from giving or accepting invitations. It's normal for teenagers to be flush one week and broke the next.

If you're doing the inviting, you can use certain words and phrases to signal your intentions. For example, if you plan on paying, you can say:

"My treat."

"Would you be my guest for...?"

"I just got my birthday money, and I'd love to take you to...."

If you don't have the bucks, you can mention that you'll have to go Dutch. Or you might say, "I can cover the tickets if you can spring for the food."

If you're on the receiving end of the invitation, don't be embarrassed about asking who pays. If money isn't an issue, you can just bring some to cover your own expenses should the need arise. If it is an issue, say, "I'd love to go, but I'm short on funds right now." That will bring things out into the open.

SPOTLIGHT ON...

GOING DUTCH

"Going Dutch" doesn't mean dining in Amsterdam. It means that each person pays his or her own share of the bill.

The tricky thing is, if you're invited out, how do you know if it's Dutch or not?

If you're lucky, the person will make it clear by saying, "Let's have dinner together Saturday, my treat," or, "I have some good news and some bad news. The good news is I'm inviting you to go out to dinner with me. The bad news is I'm flat broke, and we'll have to go Dutch."

If you're not sure who's paying, you can:

■ wait and see, being sure to have enough money with you in case you need to cover your share, or

■ say, "I'd love to go, but I'm out of funds until next Friday." The other person will say either, "Oh, that doesn't matter, I'm paying," or, "Why don't we wait 'til then, okay?"

If you do go Dutch, split the bill evenly. This saves endless hassles over who had coffee and whose appetizer cost 35 cents more. If, however, you know that your share came to much more than your date's, you should insist on putting more money in.

Being Asked Out

Someone you know has just asked you out. It's Decision Time! What you say and how you say it will depend on whether you like the person, whether you like the person enough to go out with him or her, whether you're free to date, and about a zillion other things. But basically, your answer will be "Yes," "Maybe," or "No." Let's look at the etiquette of each.

If your answer is "Yes"...

Shout it from the rooftops of your heart. Say:

> "I'd love to!"
> "That sounds great!"
> "I've always wanted to do that!"
> "I really hoped you'd ask me!"

Express enthusiasm, appreciation, anticipation, eagerness, and anything else you can think of along those lines. The person who asked you probably sweated bullets for three weeks before popping the question. He or she deserves more than:

"Okay."
"Sure."
"I guess."
"Why not?"

TIP: Never accept an invitation and back out later unless there's an emergency or you become ill. It's not fair to leave your date high and dry. He or she might have already made arrangements, spent money, or told other people. Your reversal might be inconvenient and/or embarrassing. And it would give you a reputation for being hurtful and unreliable.

If your answer is "Maybe"...

Sometimes you'll need to check with your parents or reschedule a conflict before you can accept an invitation. If this is the case, express your enthusiasm, just as you would if you answered "Yes." Then, in a verbal footnote, explain the catch. Let the person know when you'll have a definite answer. Don't invent a fake excuse to keep someone on hold for days while you wait to see if a better offer comes along.

If your answer is "No"...

There are three types of no:

1. **The "I'm-hoping-someone-else-will-ask-me" no.**
   Let's say you've been invited to a school dance by
   someone you feel lukewarm about. You're hoping
   someone else will ask you. You can't say, "I'm holding
   out for someone better," or, "I'll go with you if no one
   else asks," because that would hurt the person's feelings. And you can't say, "Sorry, but I'm going to be
   away that weekend," because then, if you turn up at
   the dance, you'll be caught in your lie. So there's only
   one thing you can say, and that is:

   > "I'm sorry, but I already have plans for Saturday. Thank you
   > for asking."

   If you show up at the dance with someone else, it'll
   be obvious what those other plans were.
   It would be rude for anyone to ask what your plans
   are. If this happens, you're under no obligation to
   respond. Just be a parrot and repeat what you said
   about already having other plans. Eventually, the
   person will give up.

2. **The "I'd-love-to-but-I-can't" no.** The key here is to
   make sure the person knows that you really want to be
   asked again. When you refuse the invitation, make sure
   you communicate your regret, dismay, disappoint-
   ment, and heartbreak:

"Oh, Nigel, I'm soooo sorry, but that's the night I volunteer at the animal shelter. But please ask me again. I'd love to go some other time."

3. **The "I-wouldn't-go-out-with-you-for-a-billion-dollars" no.** The first time someone in this category asks you out, you can use the "I already have plans" response, or, "Thank you, but I'm not free that evening." Be polite. There's no need to carve the person's feelings into mincemeat by saying, "Are you kidding? What makes you think I would *ever* go out with you?"

The second time this person asks you out (which may occur then and there—"Well, how about next Saturday?"), you can respond in the same way. If, after several refusals, he or she still doesn't take the hint, you'll need to be more direct, but in a gentle, considerate manner:

"I'm very flattered that you keep asking me, but I just don't see us going out together."

If the person presses you for a reason, make it an "I" and not a "You":

"I'm just not the person for you."

"I'm interested in someone else."

"I'm not dating anyone these days."

This type of response accomplishes two good things. First, it respects the other person's feelings. And second, it closes the door to more tries. Only someone who's completely clueless will keep asking after that.

Finally, don't blab. If you asked someone out and got turned down, you'd feel hurt or disappointed. Imagine how much worse you'd feel if the person went around telling everybody. There's not much you can do to stop others from indulging in such rudeness. But you can make sure that you never do it yourself.

Breaking Up

You've been going with the same person for a month (or a week, or a year). For whatever reason—boredom, a new love on the horizon, changing interests, incompatibility, unhappiness—you think it's time to break up. But you're a thoughtful, sensitive individual, and you'd rather not trash the other person in the process.

What's the best way to behave?

It's kind of you to ask. Whether you wish to break off all contact or redefine the relationship as "just friends," the technique is the same:

1. **Do it face-to-face.** This will be difficult, but you probably did other things face-to-face. Don't send a friend, a letter, or an email. Find a private moment when you can speak without an audience.

2. **Don't accuse or blame.** Saying, "You never pay any attention to me," or, "I'm fed up with your drinking," gives the other person the chance to say, "You're misjudging me," or, "I'll change!"

3. **Avoid making a case.** You want the breakup to seem fated, not the result of anyone's behavior. Simply say, "I want to go out with other people," or, "I guess I just don't feel the way I used to." Make it clear that your feelings have changed and you're responsible for them. It's not the other person's fault.

There's no magic formula for breaking up. Ending a relationship can be messy and painful. But if you do it quickly, directly, and decisively, you'll lessen the suffering and may even stay friends.

Teens Want to Know: A Dating Q&A

What's the best way to ask someone to dance? Do you have to go through with a blind date? How can you tell someone you're not interested in him—in a nice way?

Today's teenagers want answers to these questions and more. Unless you know everything there is to know about dating, this chapter is for you, too.

Q: What if you're not ready to date, but you just want to show a girl that you like her?

A: If you're seven years old, pull her pigtails and put a spider in her lunch box. If you're older, try these ideas:

PAY ATTENTION TO HER. Smile. Say "Hello!" Ask questions about her classes, friends, family, interests, and experiences. Showing interest in another person says, "I like you."

SPEND TIME WITH HER. Do things together. Walk with her between classes. Carry her books. Call her on the phone. Wanting to be with someone says, "I like you."

TREAT HER WITH RESPECT. Say "Please" and "Thank you." Show pleasure in her accomplishments. Comfort her when she's disappointed. Never say anything behind her back that you wouldn't say to her face. Being supportive and trustworthy says, "I like you."

BE THOUGHTFUL. Bring her a flower. Write a note. Listen carefully to everything she says. Give her a small gift that follows up on an offhanded remark she makes. Being sensitive and attentive says, "I like you."

GET THE WORD OUT. Have *your* friends let *her* friends know that you like her. This is the sort of thing that makes school so interesting.

TELL HER! The direct approach works wonders. Say, "I really like you." If that seems too forward, say, "I really like being with you," or, "I really like it when we do things together."

Q: Is it okay to go out with someone if your friend likes him, too?

A: If your friend is currently going out with him, no. If neither of you is seeing him, talk to your friend before taking any action. It's hard to stay friends when you're both competing for the same boy.

You might try to find out how the boy feels about you and your friend. If he doesn't like either of you, or he just likes one of you, knowing that might save you some time and trouble. If he likes both of you, negotiate with your friend about the best way to proceed. *Example:* You might decide that the person who's liked him the longest gets first dibs.

Sometimes sensitive teens hold back from going out with their friends' ex-boyfriends or crush objects. But you should never ask anyone to do this. It's hard enough to manage your own social life without trying to run the social lives of others.

Q: How can you let someone know you're not interested in him without hurting his feelings?

A: If he's asking you out, the simplest way to deflect his affection is by being "busy." Say:

"I'm sorry, but I have plans for that night."

If he asks again, respond with the same statement. If he calls, say:

"I'm sorry, but I'm busy and can't talk."

It should soon become clear that there's nowhere in your life to squeeze him in. If he still won't get a clue ("Is there *any* time in the next five years when you don't have plans?"), say:

"I'm afraid I'm just too busy to have much of a social life."

Of course, he'll eventually realize that you find time to go out with other guys. So a feeling of rejection is unavoidable. But etiquette doesn't erase hurt from the face of the earth; it merely tries to minimize it. And those who refuse to take face-saving hints only open themselves up to greater hurt.

Q: When you pick up your date, do you have to go up to her door, or can you sit in your car and honk until she comes out?

A: Etiquette says, "Young man, get out of that car!" A gentleman *always* goes to the door the first time he picks up a young lady at her home—and, if he's smart, on future dates as well.

He does it on the first date for three reasons:

1. so the girl's parents can meet him

2. as a sign of respect for his date

3. so he can wear a T-shirt that says, "I Met My Girlfriend's Parents and Survived"

He does it on later dates for three reasons:

1. so the girl's parents can get to know him

2. as a sign of respect for his date

3. so his date's younger siblings can wrestle with him while he's waiting for her to finish getting ready

The *only* time it's acceptable to sit in your car and honk is when you're running late. In that case, roll down your car window so when your date's parents open the door and look out, you can shout, "Sorry, I'd visit if I could, but if we don't hurry, we'll miss the first act of the opera!"

Q: When you're on a date at a restaurant, is it okay to share food?

A: Ask first. Better yet, wait until your date asks or offers to share. Don't just reach across the table.

If he's slow to offer and his onion rings look especially crisp and delicious, you might casually say, "Those rings look awesome. How are they? By the way, want some of my fries?"

Although it's rude to pass mashed potatoes from one person's mouth to another in public, it's usually okay to share some types of food at restaurants.

If it's served family-style in communal dishes—sesame shrimp, pizza, big bowls of pasta—then it's meant to be shared.

In fancy restaurants, where everyone oohs and aahs and you think "Six bucks!" every time you take a bite, you may put a taste of food on your fork and pass it to your date. If it's a first date, samples should be delivered on *his* fork.

If you plan to go halvesies on two entrées or split one, tell the waiter when you order. Many restaurants will divide food for you in the kitchen.

Q: If somebody sets you up on a blind date and you meet the person and don't like her, is it okay not to go through with the date?

A: No. That would be rude and hurtful. You can, however, take certain steps to minimize the awkwardness:

- Only go on blind dates in a group. This doesn't mean that you audition four hopefuls at once. Instead, it means that you go out with several other couples or friends. Then it's not just you and your date, in case it isn't great.

- Pick an activity that doesn't force you to talk or stare into each other's eyes all night. A movie, ice-skating, or a football game all fit the bill.

A blind date can be fun and interesting if you go with the right attitude. At best, it can result in a wonderful new friend. At worst, it's a great chance to practice your patience, tolerance, and charm.

Q: How do you deal with adults who ask, "So, is there a special little girlfriend in your life?"

A: You mean, how do you deal with nosy, obnoxious, rude adults?

You have three choices:

1. You can make a snappy comeback.

2. You can reply politely.

3. You can assert yourself without being rude.

Let's look at examples of all three in action:

1. **Snappy Comeback.** You say,  "No, unfortunately, there's no special little girlfriend in my life. Is there one in *yours?*" The adult turns red in the face and sputters off. You might experience a moment of satisfaction, but you've created an uncomfortable situation, and you've behaved disrespectfully— just like the adult.

2. **Polite Reply.** You smile and say, "I'm blessed with many friends, both girls and boys." Hidden within your reply, deep enough to guard you from accusations of disrespect but shallow enough to be felt by the adult, is this message: *None of your business.*

3. **Courteous Assertiveness.** You get to choose from a menu of possible responses, including but not limited to these:

   "Excuse me?"

   "I beg your pardon?"

   "I must have heard you wrong."

   "Isn't that kind of a personal question?"

When responding to ill-mannered questions and remarks, keep these three principles in mind:

1. You don't have to answer a nosy question just because it was asked.

2. The *least* effective response to rudeness is more rudeness.

3. The *most* effective response to rudeness is impeccable politeness.

Q: How do you ask someone to dance?

A: You say, "May I have this dance?" You don't say, "Wanna dance?" unless you're willing to hear, "Sure, but not with you!"

Q: How do you refuse if someone asks you to dance and you don't want to?

A: Believe it or not, this is trickier than doing the asking. First, you never *refuse.* You *decline,* which is more polite. You do this by claiming one of the following:

1. A physical incapacity. As in:

"I'm sorry, but...
...I'm feeling a bit tired right now."
...I'm just too overheated."
...I think I slipped a disk on that last dance."

Honor demands that for the next 10–15 minutes, you act like someone who is too tired, overheated, or out of alignment to dance. Only then can you return to the dance floor.

2. An urgent mission elsewhere. As in:

"I'm sorry, but...

...I simply must get some air."

...I have to make a phone call."

...I'd like to freshen up a bit."

You will need to disappear for a few moments to uphold your integrity.

3. A prior obligation. As in:

"I'm sorry, but...

...I promised this dance to someone else."

...I told Mrs. Lilliliver I'd help with the punch."

...I said I'd show Mindy how to do the tango."

You're probably wondering why, if someone asks you to dance, you can't just say, "No, thank you." Picture this:

You say: *"May I have this dance?"*
The other person says: *"No, thank you."*
You think: *"What th'...?"*

And you stand there for a minute or two—hurt, perplexed, not knowing what to say. Then you slink away wondering, "Why not? Is there something wrong with me? Am I too sweaty? Is it my dancing? Should I ask again?"

In other words, a polite excuse—even if it's not really true—allows both parties to maintain their dignity and self-respect. And that's the essence of good manners.

Q: If you've danced with someone once but you don't want to dance with them again, how do you get rid of them?

A: What—you don't want to go steady based on one dance? Oh, all right, be that way.

But seriously: Use the same strategies you would to decline a dance in the first place. The only difference is that you excuse yourself from the field rather than the sidelines. Thank your partner for the dance, then declare a physical incapacity, an urgent mission elsewhere, or a prior commitment. You might also smile warmly, say, "Thank you for the dance. Excuse me," and then make your exit.

Q: How do you get even with your girlfriend after she dumps you, and she has her best friend tell you instead of doing it herself?

A: First, you have every right to feel hurt and angry. Being dumped is no fun. The fact that your ex had a friend do her dirty work makes it even worse. That was just plain rude.

If you *really* want to get even in a way that your ex and her friends and all of your friends will never forget, do this: Be perfectly polite. Show that your poise and confidence don't depend on any relationship.

If you fly into a rage or badmouth your ex, you'll be playing into her hands. She might even say, "See—that's why I didn't tell him myself. I knew he'd get ugly." Other girls may think twice about going out with you.

So stay calm, be philosophical, and radiate understanding. If friends press you for a response, you can say:

"People change. Life goes on."

"I'll always cherish the memories of our time together."

"I wish her all the best in her future relationships."

Your good manners will shine a light on your ex's bad manners. When she learns how "well" you're taking it, she'll probably feel low, cowardly, and guilty, proving once again that politeness is the best revenge.

P.S. When you get home, by all means, rant, rave, and pound your pillow. Cry yourself to sleep. Talk things through with a best friend. But then get back on the horse. Stay active and involved. Don't let yourself get isolated. Spend time with your friends. Do something nice for yourself. Your friends will admire you for the stoic, upbeat way you carry on with a broken heart. Keep it up, and you may find yourself in a new relationship sooner than you think.

Q: How can you tell if you're in an abusive relationship?

A: You know when someone treats you right: You feel valued and respected and cared for. But it's not so easy to know when someone treats you wrong.

Teenagers are often confused about what's normal or acceptable in a relationship. Those who grow up in a home with two adults who love and respect each other have a model for what a healthy relationship looks like. Those who grow up in a home with parents who fight a lot may think that's normal. And those who grow up with abusive adults may not have a clue about what's normal, healthy, and respectful.

If you're wondering about your relationship and you want to understand it better, here are some questions you can ask yourself. They apply to any relationship and can be asked by boys or girls.

16 Questions to Ask Yourself If You're Wondering About Your Relationship

Does your boyfriend or girlfriend...

1. put you down in front of other people?

2. tease or embarrass you in front of other people?

3. trash your ideas?

4. ignore your feelings?

5. badmouth people or things you care about?

6. use alcohol or other drugs as an excuse for his/her behavior?

7. try to cut you off from your friends?

8. take things out on you?

9. get angry at you when you don't know why?

10. treat you poorly, apologize, promise he/she'll never do it again—then do it again?

11. blame you for things he/she has done?

12. deny that he/she has hurt you?

13. make it clear that he/she calls the shots?

14. threaten or intimidate you to get his/her way?

15. use physical force or violence against you?

16. make you engage in sexual activity you don't enjoy or aren't ready for?

If you answered yes to one or more of these questions, it means that you're almost certainly in an abusive relationship. Of course, an otherwise wonderful, loving person might have the *one* annoying habit of telling embarrassing stories about you in public, or the *one* flaw of being slightly bossy from time to time. A caring boyfriend or girlfriend, if told that his or her behavior upsets you, will make a sincere effort to respect your needs and feelings. So you'll have to use your judgment in deciding how these issues apply to your situation.

In general, though, answering yes to these questions suggests that you're in trouble. Abuse can be emotional or psychological as well as physical. If you think you might be in an abusive relationship, get help. Talk to your parents, a teacher, or a school counselor, or contact a teenage or domestic violence hotline. Another person's bad behavior is never your fault. And you don't have to take it anymore.

Sex-Ediquette

Most etiquette books steer clear of sex. That's because the behavior of consenting adults in the privacy of their bedrooms is their own business. But this is not most etiquette books.

Should teenagers be sexually active? That's not our topic here. What you decide for yourself is up to you and your partner. Your decision will depend on your values, maturity, religious beliefs, self-image, aspirations, and personal morals. It will depend on what your parents have taught you, what you've learned on your own, and ultimately what you feel is right for you.

Your decision should *not* depend on what your friends think, what your boyfriend or girlfriend wants, or what the advertising media tell you in the mixed messages they send.

Now that we've made these disclaimers, let's focus on what *is* our topic here: the etiquette related to sex.

Making Out in Public

You're waiting at a bus stop with your boyfriend, and the bus isn't due for another ten minutes. You kiss him, he kisses you back, and nine minutes later you come up for air—and dirty looks from the other people at the bus stop.

You might ask, "Why is it rude to make out in public? With all the violence in the world, what's wrong with showing a little love?" Good questions. But the fact remains that what you call "showing love," others call "inappropriate behavior."

While affection in general is to be applauded, affection in public is to be avoided. Why? Because nobody likes a show-off. It's rude to rub people's noses in the fact that you have something they don't.

This isn't about holding hands, kissing good-bye, hugging at the train station, or strolling arm-in-arm with the one you love. It's about physical contact that's basically sexual in nature. The kind that makes your heart beat faster and your blood pressure rise. (And that's just for the people who are watching.) Things like petting. Tongue wrestling. Rounding the bases between first and home.

Making out is a wonderful thing to do with someone you care about. But it should be done in private. When you do it in public, you force people to witness behavior that may be distracting or discomforting. And that, as you know, violates the basic principles of etiquette.

My boyfriend is a terrible kisser. Is there a polite way to tell him this?

No. How would you feel if he told *you* something similar? If you enjoy his company in other ways, if you're a good match in terms of your personalities and interests, then you can probably assume that he wants to please you.

Use his desire as a teaching tool. Don't say, "Ewwww!" or, "You kiss like a fish." Instead, say, "I love it when..." or, "Do you think you could...?"

On the other hand, if he has no desire to please you, it might be time to send him out to pasture. ◆

Being Discreet

If you've dated, you've had this experience: You go out with someone, and the next day all of your friends ask nosy questions. Like "How far did you get?" and "Did you _____?"

It's not surprising that your friends would feel they have the right to know such intimate details. After all, look at the bad example set by politicians who feel they have the right to legislate people's love lives. Nevertheless, you have the right to privacy. So when your friends pry into your personal affairs, smile and reply:

"A gentleman/lady never tells."

"I prefer not to discuss things of that nature."

"I can't imagine why you would be interested in things of such a personal nature."

The more secretive you sound, the more—or less— they'll assume you did. But you can't be held responsible for other people's assumptions.

Being Prepared

When a couple decides to have sex, who's supposed to bring the condom?

It doesn't matter, as long as a condom is present and properly used. No teenager today who chooses to be sexually active should have intercourse or oral sex without protection.

Traditionally, the man brought the condom. This goes back to the days when men were supposed to make the first move in a sexual relationship. Women weren't supposed to admit to having sex, much less buy condoms. That would have caused a scandal. Today, this tradition no longer makes sense. Sexually active women should have their own stash of condoms.

Unless partners have established a clear division of responsibilities—for example, one brings the condoms and the other brings the breath mints—it's the responsibility of *both* partners to ensure that they take every precaution, every time, to protect themselves and each other against pregnancy and/or disease.

What if one partner (usually the male) decides that he doesn't want to use a condom? (Because it's "not natural." It "cuts down on sensitivity." It "feels weird." It "cramps his style." Whatever.) And what if he insists that he doesn't need to use one because he's sure he doesn't have HIV/AIDS?

More lies have been told to get someone into bed than for any other reason. The only person who can be certain that he (or she) doesn't have HIV/AIDS is someone who has *never* had sex, shared needles, received a blood transfusion, or otherwise exchanged bodily fluids with another person. Anyone who has *ever* engaged in *any* of those activities, or who's mother had AIDS when he (or she) was born, could be carrying the HIV virus. He (or she) could even be carrying it if he just had a test saying he was HIV-negative! This is because it can take some time before the virus is detectable.

Most people who are HIV-positive don't know it. People who say they couldn't possibly have HIV/AIDS may be speaking the truth, or they may be deluded, in denial, or ignorant of the facts. If someone had sex just once with just one person, he or she could have acquired the virus. If, five years ago, two friends cut their palms with a pocketknife and shook hands to signify everlasting friendship, one of them could have acquired the virus from the other.

Even if both partners don't have HIV/AIDS, condoms offer added protection against pregnancy and other sexually transmitted diseases. It's a mark of good manners to do whatever one can to make a sexual partner feel comfortable and safe.

20 COMMANDMENTS
OF SEXUAL ETIQUETTE

THOU SHALT...

1. treat your partner with respect and kindness

2. make every effort to be honest in your relationship

3. be sensitive to your partner's wishes and signals, and go no further or faster than your partner wants to go

4. always use condoms and other forms of protection to reduce the risk of disease and/or pregnancy

5. refrain from blabbing intimate details about your relationship

20 COMMANDMENTS
OF SEXUAL ETIQUETTE

THOU SHALT NOT...

6. give someone the HIV virus

7. give someone any other type of sexually transmitted infection or disease

8. get someone pregnant

9. trick someone into getting you pregnant

10. bring a child into the world before you're fully able to care for it, or expect society or your parents to assume the responsibility for such a child

11. pressure someone into having sex

12. force someone to do sexual things that make him or her uncomfortable

13. use alcohol or other drugs to weaken someone's resistance or awareness

14. ignore the word "No"

15. use, abuse, and lose someone

16. say things you know aren't true just to get someone into bed

17. spill intimate secrets or spread sexual rumors

18. have sex with your best friend's partner

19. sexually harass someone

20. make rude comments about someone's body or sexual performance

BONUS CHAPTER

Aren't Manners Sexist?

They certainly are. Why should men have to take off their hats indoors while women get to keep theirs on? It's not fair!

Manners reflect the values, beliefs, and traditions of a society. These include attitudes toward social standing, age, sexuality, and the proper place of women, men, and children.

Over the centuries, many cultures have viewed women as weaker and in more need of protection than men. This doesn't mean that all the men sat around a campfire toasting marshmallows one afternoon 15,000 years ago and said,

"How can we discriminate against women?" Sex roles developed out of necessity. It made more sense for men to go out to hunt wild boars while women stayed home and had babies.

Soon, though, humans evolved. They discovered farming. Men no longer had to roam the forests, hunting and shouting "Ugh!" But instead of staying home, they went in search of new worlds to conquer. Armies of men crossed whole continents to wage war. Meanwhile, the women stayed home.

As history marched on, rules of chivalry developed. These rules governed the behavior of men toward women. The rules were based on principles of medieval knighthood, such as honor, bravery, protecting the weak, and not standing outside in your armor during a lightning storm. A gallant gentleman always treated the "fairer" (that is, weaker) sex with deference and respect. He would stand when a lady entered or left a room, defend her honor, hold doors, tip his hat, and offer his cloak.

These rules of etiquette led to many of the gender-based manners popular at the start of the 20th century. A gentleman would offer his seat to a lady, carry the luggage, pay the tab, drive the car, earn the money, and run the roost. Women were forbidden by custom and law from doing all sorts of things. In fact, women in the United States couldn't even vote until 1920!

Happily, times have changed, and the role of women in America (and many other countries) has been transformed over the past several decades. Women now hold office, run corporations, drive buses, preach sermons, remove organs, fly planes, wear pants with flies, and drop bombs. Girls can ask boys for dates. Enlightened people no longer believe that women are "weak" and "inferior."

Women's rights have been won only after years of struggle, protest, and legal challenge. Manners are even slower to change because they are passed from older to younger generations. We are now in a period of great flux in terms of defining proper behavior between men and women. Attitudes and actions that were once considered polite are now considered rude or old-fashioned.

By today's standards, certain rules of etiquette are sexist. They are based on untrue and discriminatory ideas about women's nature and role. But manners, by definition, should not, and need not, be sexist. Kindness knows no gender.

Aren't men supposed to walk on the outside of women?

No. Walking on women is never proper. However, there is a tradition of men walking on the outside of the *sidewalk* when escorting women down the street.

In olden days, this gave women some protection against slop from above and slush from below. Streets weren't paved. People went to the bathroom during the night in chamber pots, which they dumped out their windows in the morning. Apparently it was better if the contents landed on men's heads.

Now *that's* sexist. ◆

INDEX

A

Abusive relationships, 100–102
Adults
  confiding in, 71, 72–73
  correcting, 28
  introductions and, 15, 16–17
  meeting dates of teens, 92–93
  questions about dating from,
    94–96
Affection, showing in public, 104
AIDS, 107
Alcohol
  abusive relationships and, 101
  conversations and, 24
  driving and, 53–55
  refusing, 51–53
  sex etiquette and, 109
Apologizing
  in abusive relationships, 101
  tips for, 59
  when not to, 38

B

Backbiting. *See* Badmouthing
Badmouthing
  abusive relationships and, 100
  breaking up and, 98–99
  by friends, 22–23, 55–57, 60–61
Blind dates, 94
Blind people, 44
Body language
  communicating with, 22, 25
  when being introduced, 12
Bragging, 31–32
Breaking up, 87–88, 98–99

C

Chivalry, rules of, 112
Cliques, 41–42
  See also Groups

Commandments of sexual etiquette,
  108–109
Compliments, 40
Condoms, 106–107, 108
Congratulations, accepting, 32
Conversations
  body language and, 22, 25
  correcting others during, 28–29
  drinking and, 24
  emotional content of, 26–27
  ending, 32–35, 64–65
  informational content of, 25–26
  interrupting others during,
    29–31, 35
  keeping going, 22
  listening in on, 27–28
  with people with disabilities, 31,
    44–45, 46–48
  polite listening and, 24–27
  rules of courteous, 22–23, 24
  starting, 8, 13, 19–22
Corrections, 28–29

D

Dances, 96–98
Dates and dating. *See* Romance
Deaf people, 44
Debt dodgers, 63–64
Disabled people. *See* People with
  disabilities (PWDs)
Drinking
  abusive relationships and, 101
  conversations and, 24
  driving and, 53–55
  refusing, 51–53
  sex etiquette and, 109
Driving and drinking, 53–55
Drugs
  abusive relationships and, 101

ABOUT THE AUTHOR

Alex J. Packer (but you may call him "Alex") is a very polite educator and psychologist who only drinks from the carton if nobody's watching. He is the author of the award-winning *How Rude!™ The Teenagers' Guide to Good Manners, Proper Behavior, and Not Grossing People Out; HIGHS! Over 150 Ways to Feel Really, REALLY Good… Without Alcohol or Other Drugs; Bringing Up Parents: The Teenager's Handbook; Parenting One Day at a Time;* and other titles. His books have been translated into Spanish, German, and Chinese, although Alex says he can't tell if the Chinese version is really his book or a guide to lawnmower repair. His articles have appeared in *McCall's, Child, U.S. News and World Report,* and the *Harvard Graduate School of Education Bulletin.*

Alex prepped at Phillips Exeter Academy, where he never once referred to kitchen personnel as "wombats" (although he *was* told to get a haircut by his dorm master). He then went to Harvard, where he pursued a joint major in Social Relations and Finger Bowls, always striving to avoid classes on Mondays or Fridays. A specialist in adolescence, parent education, and substance abuse, Alex received a Master's Degree in Education from the Harvard Graduate School of (duh) Education, and a Ph.D. in Educational and Developmental Psychology from Boston College, where he held doors for his professors.

For eight years, Alex was headmaster of an alternative school for children ages 11–15 in Washington, D.C. He has since served as Director of Education for the Capital Children's Museum. He is currently President of FCD Educational Services, a leading Boston-based provider of drug education and prevention services for schools worldwide. When asking kids to not use drugs, Alex always says "please."

Although it's rude to talk behind someone's back, reliable sources report that Alex writes screenplays, spends several months a year in France, lives in a loft that used to be a pillow factory, and chews with his mouth closed.

Other Great Books from Free Spirit